ROAMING
DORK WEASEL

Coloring Book for Immature Adults

janet schwind

Schwind Design Shop

Published by Schwind Design Shop,
the official creative/publishing arm of B.G. Global LLC.
janetschwind@gmail.com

Please enjoy this keyword-riddled non-fiction freehand-sketched creative coloring book for adults, which will provide you with hours and hours of art therapy and the calming effects of this focused, relaxing form of self-help creativity.

These are drawings done the old-fashioned artist way—by hand, and freehand, meaning I almost never plan them in pencil but create as I go. Any imperfections are a part of the natural fabric of my overcaffeinated, undigital drawing style.

Special thanks go to my dear colleague and friend Suzanne Parada, ParadaDesign.com, for her excellent, generous and patient layout/design of this coloring book. As an independent graphic designer, Suzanne has collaborated with me on hundreds of book projects over the past ten years, she as designer and me as editor. I couldn't have done this without her!

What is a dork weasel?

According to the Urban Dictionary, a dork is someone who has odd interests, and is often silly at times. Others say a dork is nerdy, slow, dim-witted, or socially inept. A dork is also someone who can be themselves and not care what anyone thinks. A dork weasel, then, is a step beyond—much like a dork weed—but personified by a furry, energetic little predator.

This coloring book, my first, is dedicated to my beloved brother Dougie, the self-proclaimed alpha dork of our family and child number four of six. Dougie lost his year-long battle with lung cancer on January 13, 2018, and we miss him dearly.

As my older brother, Dougie showed me what it truly meant to be a dork. There will never be anyone like Dougie—he was unique and funny and dorky and he loved being different. We love him for all those reasons. The world became less interesting when we lost him.

When he was not fist-pumping in celebration of something dorky he just said or did, he was probably doing something predatory involving food—thinking about food, thinking about making food, or buying food, or hunting food, or processing meat into food form, or scooping up roadkill to give as a gift. He wanted to start a restaurant called Roadkill Café—"You kills 'em and we cooks 'em and you eats 'em!"

We Schwinds revel in our dorkiness. The title of this coloring book comes from Dougie who at one time called me a roaming dork weasel because of my frequent gypsy-like wanderings to places near and far, like my Camino pilgrimage in Spain or my weekend trips to Indianapolis. I like to think that my drawings reflect that same wandering spirit—freeform and adventurous. And you'll find a dork weasel or two roaming throughout the sketches, too.

Dougie will always be my favorite dork weasel. This coloring book celebrates Dougie and dorks and joy and hope and humor and family. I believe in using joy as a weapon. So grab your favorite coloring tools and let's bludgeon darkness with glorious coloring fun!

Anatomy of a
ROAMING DORK WEASEL

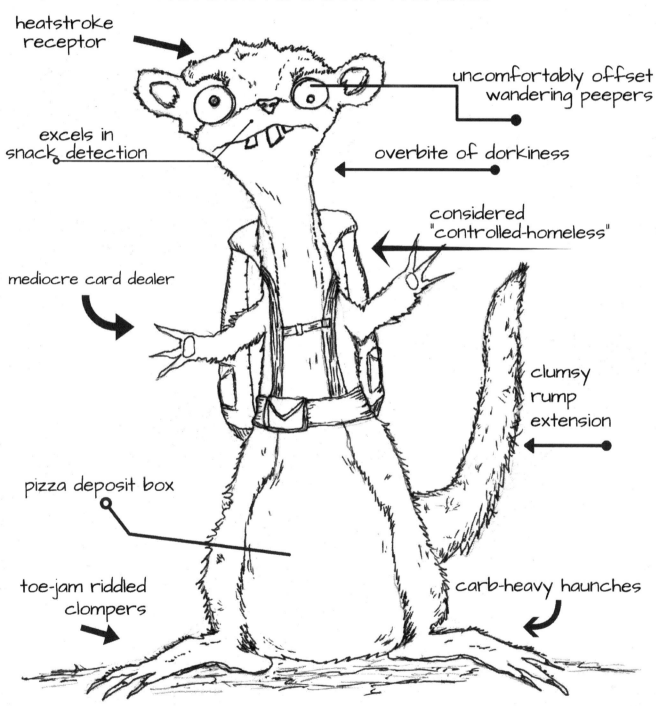

heatstroke receptor

uncomfortably offset wandering peepers

overbite of dorkiness

excels in snack detection

considered "controlled-homeless"

mediocre card dealer

clumsy rump extension

pizza deposit box

toe-jam riddled clompers

carb-heavy haunches

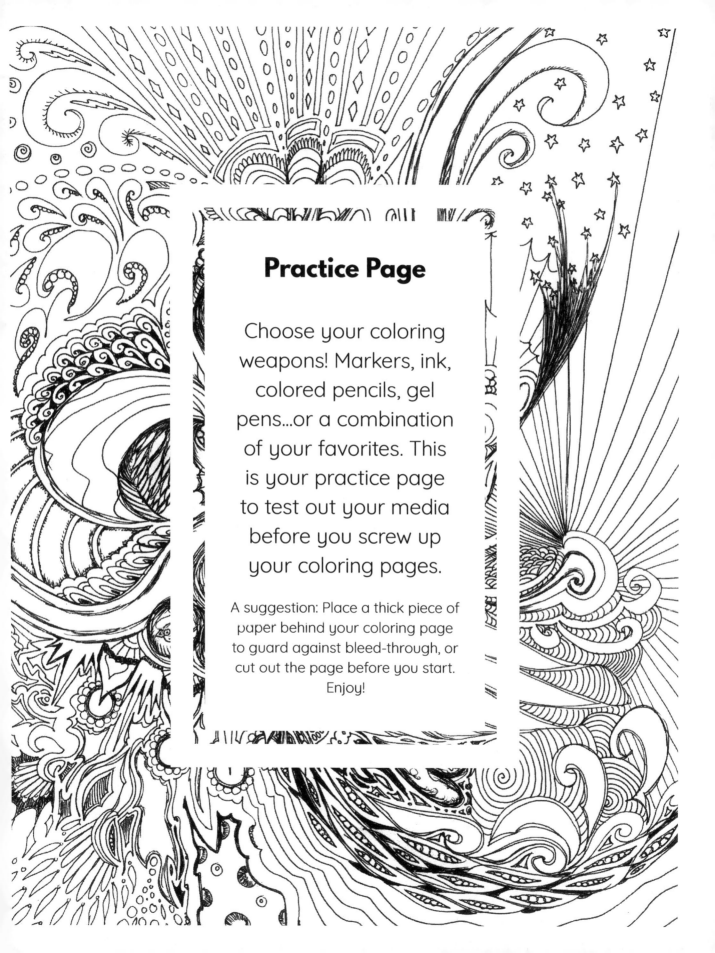

Practice Page

Choose your coloring weapons! Markers, ink, colored pencils, gel pens...or a combination of your favorites. This is your practice page to test out your media before you screw up your coloring pages.

A suggestion: Place a thick piece of paper behind your coloring page to guard against bleed-through, or cut out the page before you start. Enjoy!

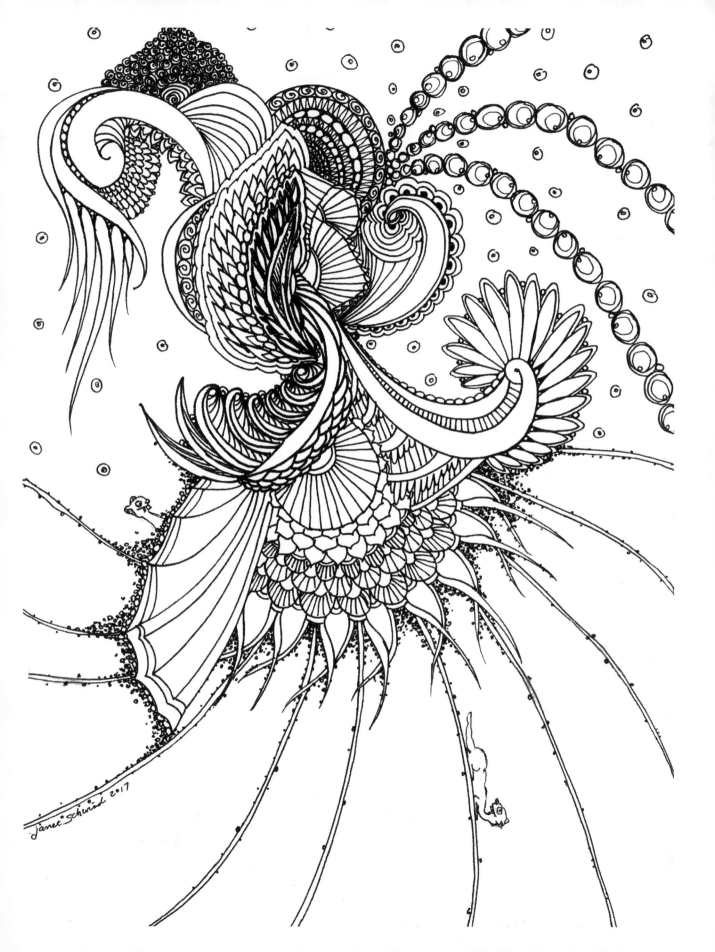

Dork Weasels in a Snowstorm

Dork Weasels in Heavy Cloud Cover

Janet Schwind is a ridiculously professional artist, writer, editor, publisher, 5-minute public speaker and Camino pilgrim. As one of six creatively gifted siblings, she grew up with a love for art, especially drawing—a talent that was passed down from her father Robert in the form of humorous pencil sketches, elegant typography, wildlife paintings, and things like mobiles made from rabbit vertebrae. Even Mom would occasionally quick-sketch her cartoon ladies in fancy hats smoking cigarettes, or her doodles of cartoon dogs with complacent human faces.

Janet always thought she would pursue art as a career until she got to college where she was discouraged in her art, lacking confidence to pursue it as a livelihood. Journalism seemed a fitting alternative as she had always loved writing, too. Art was put on the back burner for several decades as life in the advertising world snuffed out her artistic endeavors.

In 2013 Janet had an awakening after strapping on an oversized backpack and setting out an on amazing adventure to walk the ancient path called the Camino de Santiago—a 500-mile pilgrimage starting from St. Jean Pied de Port, France, and ending in Santiago de Compostela, Spain, where the apostle James's bones are enshrined.

As a result of her trek, renewing dreams and overcoming fears became Janet's new hobby. Next she conquered a lifelong phobia of public speaking—and did not die from it! She also enrolled in supernatural ministry school where she experienced a personal revival and more awakening of dreams with God, one of which you see here—creating a coloring book for immature adults, with more to come, including downloadable coloring eBooks. She also began writing a non-fiction book called Ridiculously Supernatural.

Janet is a northern Indiana native living, writing, editing and publishing books, making art again and dreaming in South Bend, Indiana. She likes writing of herself in third person.

Ways to connect with Janet:

JanetSchwind.com
facebook.com/JanetMonkeyArtShop
coroflot.com/janetschwindwritingandediting
linkedin.com/in/janetschwind/
janetschwind@gmail.com

Thanks for buying Janet's first coloring book. She'd be real grateful if you leave a review on Amazon!

Made in the USA
Las Vegas, NV
19 November 2022

59806644R00022